INTERNATIONAL AND CLASSIC FAVORITES FOR CLARINET SOLO

MB99550

BY NORMAN HEIM

Free Piano Accompaniment available online!
Visit www.melbay.com/99550

Introduction

This collection of music arranged for B-flat clarinet and piano is divided into two sections. The first has eleven folk songs from around the world that can be played by intermediate level performers (both instruments).

The second section consists of ten compositions that are well known and were written in the eighteenth and nineteenth centuries by esteemed composers such as Pachelbel, Handel, J.S. Bach, Mendelssohn and Beethoven. This music can be played by intermediate level clarinetists, and the piano accompaniments will be of moderate challenge.

The selections in each section are of moderate length and can be played for festival, church, school and leisure occasions.

Table of Contents

International Folk Songs/B flat Clarinet Solo
Shenandoah...6
My Hat has Three Corners...7
La Jesucita...8
Turkey in the Straw...10
Oh, Dear! What can the Matter Be...12
Folk Songs from Asia...13
Deep River...14
Volga Boat Song...15
Santa Lucia...16
Londonderry Air...17
When the Saints Go Marching...18

Classic Favorites/B flat Clarinet Solo
Canon...20
Jesu, Joy of Man's Desiring...22
Largo from Xerxes...24
Gavotte...25
Turkish March...26
Faith Op. 102, No. 6...27
O Lord Most Holy (Panis Angelicus)...28
Waltz in A Flat...29
Dance-Anitra Op. 46, No. 3...30
Pavane...32

International Folk Favorites

for B flat Clarinet

Shenandoah

Bb Clarinet

United States

Lento
mp
mf
mp
p
mf
dim.
mp
pp
p
mp
p
pp
pp
rit.

My Hat has Three Corners

B♭ Clarinet

Germany

La Jesucita

Turkey in the Straw

p
f
p
f
p
pp
mf
p
mf
f
p
f
p
f
dim.
rit.

Oh, Dear! What can the Matter Be

Folk Songs from Asia

B♭ Clarinet

Deep River

Spiritual, United States

14

Volga Boat Song

Santa Lucia

Londonderry Air

When the Saints Go Marching

Classical Favorites

for B flat Clarinet

Canon

B♭ Clarinet
Johann Pachelbel
Andantino (♩ = 88)
p
mp
mf
mp
mf
cresc.
f
mf
mp
cresc.
p
pp
rit.
pp
20

Jesu, Joy of Man's Desiring

B♭ Clarinet

Johann Sebastian Bach

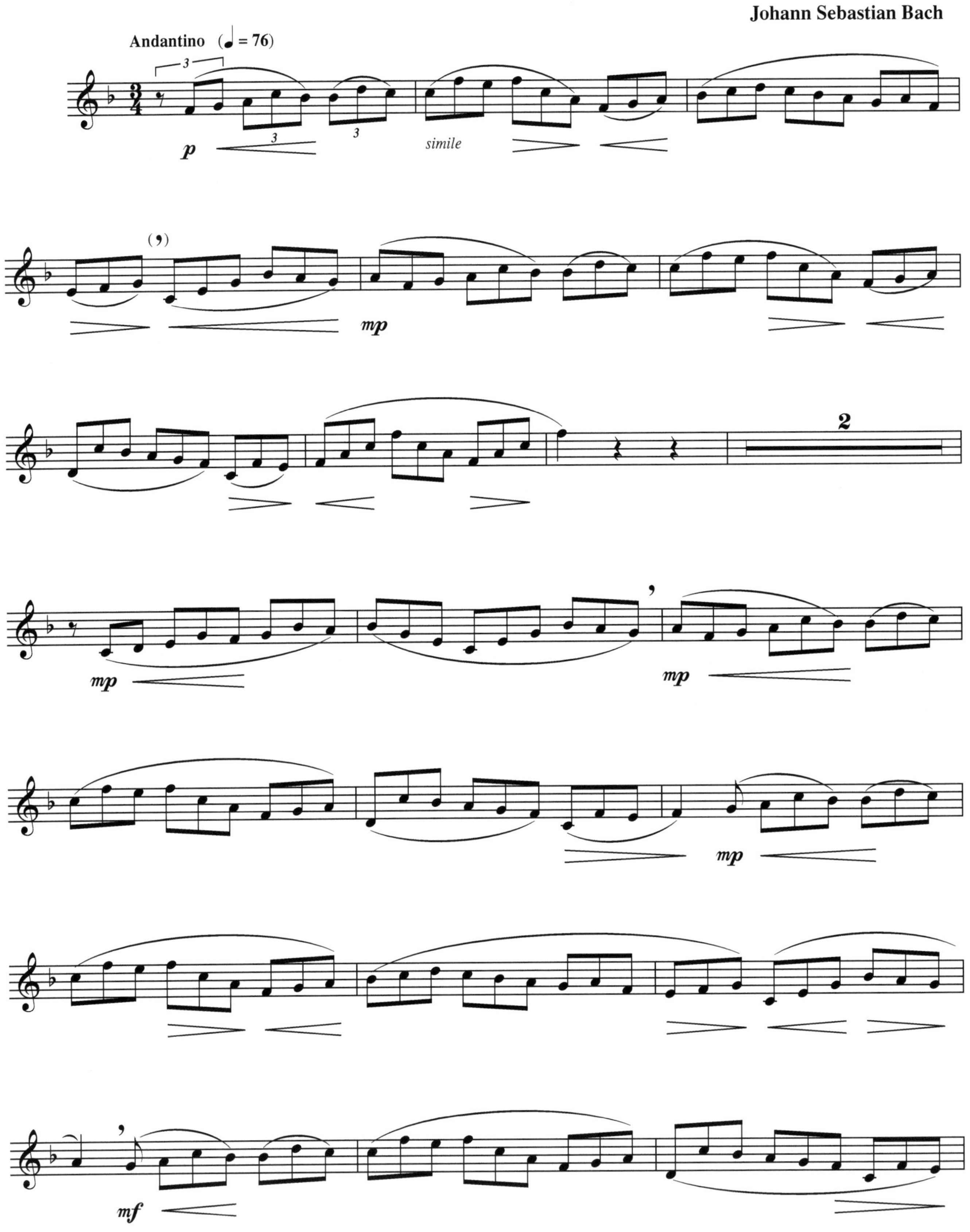

p
p
f
mf
simile dim.
p
rit.
pp

Largo from Xerxes

B♭ Clarinet

Georg F. Handel

24

Gavotte

Bb Clarinet
E. J. Gossec
Allegretto (♩ = 112)
p
mp
cresc.
mf
p
cresc.
f
p
f
mp
p
mf
p
cresc.
p
mp
pp
p
cresc.
f
p
cresc.
f

Turkish March

Faith Op. 102, No. 6

O Lord Most Holy
(Panis Angelicus)

Waltz in A Flat

Dance-Anitra Op. 46, No. 3

Tempo I
rit.
3
f mf mf mf f mf p mp mf mp p pp f pp

Pavane

B♭ Clarinet

Maurice Ravel

BILL'S
MUSIC
SHELF

UNIQUELY INTERESTING MUSIC!